# AWED & AMAZED

*A Devotional Collection for Women*

JULIA BETTENCOURT

All Scripture quotations are from the King James Bible.

The devotionals within this collection were previously published to www.juliabettencourt.com.

ISBN-13: 978-1724944283
ISBN-10: 1724944282

# DEDICATION

This book is dedicated to my dad who taught me to see the beauty in all the world around me through many a walk through the woods together.

# CONTENTS

# INTRODUCTION

I am always awed and amazed at the birds, the critters, the flowers, the trees, the wind, the oceans, and all the incredible things on earth that God has made. These beautiful things are a constant source of wisdom for me.

I hope you will enjoy reading through these devotionals and reflecting on some of the amazing wonders that the Lord has put there for us to learn from and to admire.

*O LORD, how manifold are thy works!*
*in wisdom hast thou made them all:*
*the earth is full of thy riches.  Psalm 104:24*

# 1
## FLUTTER BY!

*Therefore if any man be in Christ, he is a new creature: old things are passed away; behold, all things are become new.* *2 Corinthians 5:17*

Many times I'm inspired to write because of nature and the unique way God made something. I began thinking about the butterfly and about how it emerges into the beautiful creature that it is.

I know you've probably all heard the analogy of the butterfly and new life in Christ. I love that thought, but I was curious to know more about this little creature so I went and read up on the subject of butterflies.

I found some amazing facts about the butterfly which was just a reminder once again of how intricately God made each creature from the big huge hippopotamus down to the tiny insect. The joys of creation are everywhere!

Here are some things that stood out to me about the butterfly.

## Butterflies have predators.

As lovely as the butterfly is, there are other little creatures out there that prey on it. There are wasps, birds, snakes, and frogs to name just a few.

When we have that new life in Christ, we have a predator too. Just like the butterfly needs to be aware of his surroundings and how its predators can attack him, so do we as Christians. The devil is out there and he is seeking us out. He's our "adversary".

*Be sober, be vigilant; because your adversary the devil, as a roaring lion, walketh about, seeking whom he may devour. 1 Peter 5:8*

## Butterflies need the sun.

I read somewhere that butterflies can't fly if their temperature is less than 86°. They cannot produce heat on their own and butterflies must rely on the sun to heat up their wings in order for them to move about. They have strong muscles but they can't fly without the sun to warm their bodies first.

I used to wonder why I'd see butterflies sometimes sitting on a branch, just sitting there, almost not moving for a very long time, with maybe just a slight movement of the wings. Apparently they were soaking up the sun in order to take flight.

Wow! That is how we are as Christians. We can't do things on our own. We need the "Son" to warm us as well. We don't move along very well in our own strength. Do we? We have to rely on the Lord's strength and guidance before we can accomplish anything.

*I can do all things through Christ which strengtheneth me. Philippians 4:13*

## Butterflies can see ultraviolent light.

Did you know that the butterfly has the ability to see things we humans cannot see? They have the ability to see ultraviolent light which helps vividly guide them so they can find nectar to drink.

As Christians we have a special eyesight as well and we can see things others don't. Sometimes those without Christ just don't understand us Christians. We have the ability to see with the eyes of faith.

I think of all of those heroes of faith in Hebrews chapter 11 and all the things that happened because of their faith.

*Now faith is the substance of things hoped for, the evidence of things not seen.* *Hebrews 11:1*

## **<u>Final Thoughts</u>**

These butterfly traits make me think of David when he went to battle Goliath. He could see vividly what God was going to do. Don't you just love how David had been basking in the "Son" shine? He was ready to move for the Lord.

That big old giant was taunting David and telling him how he was going to give his flesh to the birds and the beasts, but David was seeing with those eyes of faith. I just love this passage. It's one of those that send that surge through me that says, "Yes!" God is in control.

*Then said David to the Philistine, Thou comest to me with a sword, and with a spear, and with a shield: but I come to thee in the name of the LORD of hosts, the God of the armies of Israel, whom thou hast defied. This day will the LORD deliver thee into mine hand; and I will smite thee, and take thine head from thee; and I will give the carcases of the host of the Philistines this day unto the fowls of the air, and to the wild beasts of the earth; that all the earth may know that there is a God in Israel. And all this assembly shall know that the LORD saveth not with sword and spear: for the battle is the LORD's, and he will give you into our hands. 1 Samuel 17:45-47*

My favorite part is when David says, "...I come to thee in the name of the LORD of hosts, the God of the armies of Israel...". We cannot do anything in our own strength. We sure can't "flutter" very far.

Going back to 2 Corinthians 5:17, it states,

*Therefore if any man be in Christ, he is a new creature: old things are passed away; behold, all things are become new.*

We've got to be constantly soaking up God's Word and spending time with the "Son" of God before we can move forward and take flight.

## So, how are you fluttering?

# PRETTY FLOWERS ALL IN A ROW

*And yet I say unto you, That even Solomon in all his glory was not arrayed like one of these. Matthew 6:29*

Flowers are one of the most beautiful things I think God created. Sometimes I think He created them just for me. They give me this happy feeling.

When I see how simple but yet how fantastic flowers are, I can't help thinking that God is still in control and all is right with the world.

People have loved flowers back from the beginning of time and there are different meanings that have been associated with specific ones over the years. Many flowers have come to have several different meanings. We will take a look at just four of them to see what we can learn.

**Aster means contentment.**

Asters are those pretty little dainty white flowers that have a yellow center. I think they look like wild daisies. We have them growing along the roads here in California where I live and I always think I'd like to just stop the car and get out and pick some to take home.

One of the meanings associated with the aster flower is contentment. I kind of like that. They are simple yet pretty flowers and they do give me that sense of contentment.

Those words in Philippians come to mind.

*Not that I speak in respect of want: for I have learned, in whatsoever state I am, therewith to be content. Philippians 4:11*

Contentment sure is a nice place to be in our lives. Isn't it? No matter what the circumstances we have that ease of satisfaction. The problem I think that people have with contentment is that they get it confused with being complacent.

Complacent means we don't care about things or are unconcerned, but being content is not that. When we are content, we end up caring more because we don't allow things around us to get us off track. It's being able to push forward and have that peace no matter what the circumstances.

## Camellia means graciousness.

I have a lot of favorite flowers and camellias are right there toward the top of my list. I have a large camellia bush beside my front porch. Right now they are in full bloom and are so breathtakingly beautiful. They make me smile every time I pass them.

The meaning associated with the camellia is graciousness. I think that's a word we don't hear used much anymore and we certainly don't see it displayed much. It means *excellence of manners or social conduct.*

Shouldn't we as Christian women embody that? The world sure doesn't.

You don't have to turn on the television for more than a few seconds and you'll see ads for those reality shows that have these type of women (if you can call them women) that are anything but gracious. It sickens my stomach at how proud they are of being hateful, mean, cruel, and distasteful in every sense of the word.

As Christian women, those definitely are not our role models. I think if we want to be in full bloom as Christian women we really need to concentrate on being gracious. I have known a few very gracious Christian women in my life and to me that makes them quite breathtakingly beautiful.

*A gracious woman retaineth honour... Proverbs 11:16*

## Larkspur means beautiful spirit.

The larkspur is a pretty flower. I've mostly seen them in purple but they can be other colors as well. One of the meanings associated with the larkspur is a "beautiful spirit". Wow. That's something to strive for. I love that verse in 1 Peter where it is talking about a "meek and quiet spirit". Now that is a "beautiful" spirit for a Christian lady.

*But let it be the hidden man of the heart, in that which is not corruptible, even the ornament of a meek and quiet spirit, which is in the sight of God of great price. 1 Peter 3:4*

One thing I read about the larkspur is that some

of them have become endangered and that you don't find as many anymore except for those grown specifically for flower arranging. It is kind of like those "meek and quiet spirit" ladies. There doesn't seem to be an abundance of them either.

## Black Eyed Susan means encouragement.

I have always admired the black eyed Susan. They are so bright and striking that I think they normally contrast everything around them. The meaning of the black eyed Susan is encouragement.

I sure love to be around encouraging people. Don't you? People that give you that special word you need just at that moment or are there to cheer you on in whatever you are doing at the time. Those bright people definitely contrast with those around them.

*Let no corrupt communication proceed out of your mouth, but that which is good to the use of edifying, that it may minister grace unto the hearers. Ephesians 4:29*

## <u>Final Thoughts</u>

I think there are things in our Christian lives that we have to have like pretty flowers all lined up in a row, especially things like these four — contentment, graciousness, beautiful spirits, and encouragement.

There are other things too all involved in our Christian living such as love, compassion, and all those other things Christ taught us. When we have these things in order, we have a tendency to live our Christian lives in a more beautiful way.

No one ever said that the Christian life was easy and when it comes to some of these, it requires a little work. We can't just put up our little place markers with our flower names on them and expect them to flourish if we leave them alone.

They require us to put some energy into them by using those tools of Bible study, prayer, and righteous living. I know I've got some of these things wilting in my flower box which I need to tend to a little more closely.

**So, are your flowers all in a row?**

# 3

## GOING TO THE BIRDS

*And God created great whales, and every living creature*
*that moveth, which the waters brought forth abundantly,*
*after their kind, and every winged fowl after his kind: and*
*God saw that it was good.  Genesis 1:21*

**W**e are going to the birds today to see what they can teach us, so get your binoculars and we'll go birdwatching together. We are going to see what some of those old bird-related sayings can teach us through some early birds, owls, hawks, and crows.

### *The early bird gets the worm.*

I guess you've heard that one before.  It means the first bird there is sure to get the worm and get fed.  To put it in our vernacular, to us ladies that means the first one in the store to shop gets the good deals.  Ever been shopping that day after Thanksgiving or when a big sale is going on?

Everyone is lined up at the door before the store opens, just waiting to see what they can snatch up like a bird does a worm. Look at how hard some of us try to get there early.

We go to bed early the day before, get up early, and fly off ready to swoop down. And watch out! You may get pecked on if you are holding something someone else wants.

I think that we should all have the attitude that we want to get to our Bibles first and be fed with the Word of God each morning. How early do we get up to make sure we have that time that we need in the Scriptures to get fed for the day?

Do we mind missing a little sleep to make sure we don't miss out on those wonderful blessings and nuggets that will see us through? We've got to make it a habit to get up early and snatch up some nourishment from God's Word that we will need to fortify us.

Adult birds will take a worm back to their little babies, so us moms need to remember that too. Do we dig in and share what we learn from the Word with our children?

*O God, thou art my God; early will I seek thee: my soul*

*thirsteth for thee, my flesh longeth for thee in a dry and thirsty land, where no water is. Psalm 63:1*

### Be wise as an owl.

I'm not a big fan of owls (to me they're creepy), but I sure would like to be wise. I tried to find out why they were considered wise and there were more than a few answers. Some people say that in Greek mythology the owl was associated with Athena, who was considered the goddess of wisdom.

Some sources said it was because an owl looks serious, old, and wise. Another source said it was because the owl sees all but really doesn't say much, and even another source said because large eyes are a sign of wisdom.

I really don't know if there is just one answer, but whatever the reason, I think we could all do with a little more wisdom. Solomon wanted wisdom more than anything. Wisdom is a wonderful treasure which we should be seeking too.

*Wisdom is the principal thing; therefore get wisdom: and with all thy getting get understanding. Proverbs 4:7*

*How much better is it to get wisdom than gold!*
*and to get understanding rather to be chosen*
*than silver! Proverbs 16:16*

## Watch like a hawk.

This saying means to watch someone or something very closely. Hawks have very sharp eyesight and they fly high in the air so they have a good view. They are able to easily watch for prey and keep an eye out to protect their nests.

There are some things that come into our lives that we've got to watch like a hawk too. We need to watch every area of our life that could get attacked and make us lose our witness. We've got to get that aerial view and be on the lookout for sin that could sneak in to destroy us. We have to be on guard when it comes to our Christian walk.

*Watch and pray, that ye enter not into temptation:*
*the spirit indeed is willing, but the flesh is*
*weak. Matthew 26:41*

## I have something to crow about.

This one we usually interpret as meaning we have

something to say. Usually exciting news! As Christians we do have exciting news to share about Christ. We also have an important warning that we probably don't talk about as much as we should.

Warning people of an everlasting hell seems to always be on the back burner for us Christians. The rich man in hell sure knew it was important and wanted someone to go to his family and warn them so they wouldn't end up where he was.

*Then he said, I pray thee therefore, father, that thou wouldest send him to my father's house: For I have five brethren; that he may testify unto them, lest they also come into this place of torment.   Luke 16:27-28*

We do have something to *crow* about.

## **Final Thoughts**

I hope you've enjoyed our bird watching expedition. The Lord created such wonderful creatures such as the birds for us to enjoy, but also to learn a few lessons from too.

We have a hummingbird that spends a lot of time

outside my living room window. There is a bottlebrush tree right there that he's attracted to. Sometimes he is there every day for a while. Then he disappears sometimes for a month or so and then it comes back again.

Actually, I don't know if it's just one hummingbird or if I'm enjoying several different ones over time. Anyway, I sure enjoy watching them, and every time I see them, I'm reminded how intricate and marvelous all of God's creatures are.

I have a small table with a couple chairs sitting by the window and so I can sit there with my coffee, just a couple feet away from that bird.

Sometimes it makes me sing out-loud, *How Great Thou Art!* when I see that bird looking like a little helicopter outside my window. I have to make myself turn away and get back to what I was doing as I'm so fascinated by it.

I love that the Lord gives me little things like the birds to enjoy which encourages me and makes me think. It helps me remember how wonderful a God I have.

*Thou, even thou, art LORD alone; thou hast made heaven, the heaven of heavens, with all their host, the earth, and all things that are therein, the seas, and all that is therein, and thou preservest them all; and the host of heaven worshippeth thee.  Nehemiah 9:6*

## So, are you watching for God's lessons?

# 4

## UNDER HIS WINGS

*He shall cover thee with his feathers, and*
*under his wings shalt thou trust... Psalm 91:4*

### Dig Deeper:  Read Psalm 91:1-16

Psalm 91 has always been one of my *refuge passages*. Do you have any of those? You know, those places in Scripture where we run when we need to feel loved and protected? I love the illustration of the hen covering its chicks with its feathers in verse 4 of that chapter.

When I was pretty little, my grandmother had chickens and I used to love to go there and she'd put some seed in my hand to help feed them. I can remember how it felt for her hand to touch mine and the tingly feel of that seed filling up my little hand. We weren't supposed to throw it until she said it was okay to toss it out for the chicks.

Sometimes when we'd go visit my grandparents

you wouldn't see any chicks running around. They'd be all hidden under the hens. It was always hard for me to believe that those chicks were really under there. The hens were keeping those chicks safe and warm under all those feathers. I'm so glad the Lord keeps us under His wings. It is a wonderful place to be.

## There is protection under His wings.

Being under God's wings provides such a picture of His protection to us. When David was having such difficulties in his life, where did he go? Straight to pour his heart out to the Lord. Here he was being chased by Saul who intended on killing David. He was scared and needed to find his refuge in God.

*... yea, in the shadow of thy wings will I make my refuge, until these calamities be overpast. Psalm 57:1*

## There is comfort under His wings.

When a hen gathers her chicks under her wings when it is storming or there is something that has scared the chicks, they will eventually all calm down under those wings. Being under there comforts and settles those chicks when life gets scary for them.

Growing up most of us probably longed to feel the comfort of our moms, especially when we were physically hurt or when we were hurt emotionally. Even if you grew up without a mother or didn't have the best relationship with yours, I think we all instinctively long to feel that tenderness and gentleness of a mother's comfort.

How much more with God? He is the Great Comforter.

*Blessed be God, even the Father of our Lord Jesus Christ, the Father of mercies, and the God of all comfort; Who comforteth us in all our tribulation, that we may be able to comfort them which are in any trouble, by the comfort wherewith we ourselves are comforted of God. 2 Corinthians 1:3-4*

Even as adults we go through times when things scare us. We deal with sorrow, or we even still get those boo-boos that we want to be comforted about.

We need to get up there closer under the Lord's wings and let Him comfort us.

There are ways He will gently talk to us. "It's okay". "It's alright". "Tell me about it". "Well, why don't you sleep on it". Or even, "Things will look better in the morning". If we look in His Word, it is full of tidbits of comfort for us.

## There is trust under His wings.

We know that under the Lord's wings we are able to trust Him. He's not going to fail us. He might not always provide and protect in the way that we'd choose but He has our best interests at heart.

Have you read through the book of Ruth and looked at her life? She lost her husband and ended up going to a land she wasn't familiar with. It wasn't easy for her, but the Lord had a unique way of taking care of her, and Ruth trusted Him. Boaz, who Ruth ends up marrying, recognized her trust in the Lord in Ruth chapter 2.

*And Boaz answered and said unto her, It hath fully been shewed me, all that thou hast done unto thy mother in law*

*since the death of thine husband: and how thou hast left thy*
*father and thy mother, and the land of thy nativity, and art*
*come unto a people which thou knewest not heretofore. The*
*LORD recompense thy work, and a full reward be given*
*thee of the LORD God of Israel, under whose wings thou*
*art come to trust. Ruth 2:11-12*

## There is love under His wings.

There is nothing like God's love to us. We may
have friends and relatives who we feel just don't love
us here on this earth.

Maybe some of you have even had mothers that
you felt just really didn't love you like they should
have or even loved you at all. You knew they were
supposed to be the mother hen and spread out those
wings and protect and love you but they didn't.

I know there's nothing I can say that can take
that hurt completely away from you, but know we
do have a wonderful God that loves us and it's a love
that will never fail us. Nothing can separate us from
that love either.

*Who shall separate us from the love of Christ? shall*
*tribulation, or distress, or persecution, or famine, or*

*nakedness, or peril, or sword? Romans 8:35*

*For I am persuaded, that neither death, nor life, nor angels, nor principalities, nor powers, nor things present, nor things to come, Nor height, nor depth, nor any other creature, shall be able to separate us from the love of God, which is in Christ Jesus our Lord. Romans 8:38-39*

We are so blessed that we can rest under God's wings in His love. We can know the joy that He's always there for us to tuck us under those feathers.

## There is satisfaction under His wings.

A good mother longs to satisfy the needs of her children, whether it be for food, clothing, health, or what have you. Being under God's wings satisfies us. He not only satisfies our physical needs but also our spiritual needs. He satisfies our very souls.

*How excellent is thy lovingkindness, O God! Therefore the children of men put their trust under the shadow of thy wings. They shall be abundantly satisfied with the fatness of thy house; and thou shalt make them drink of the river of thy pleasures. Psalm 36:7-8*

# There is rejoicing under His wings.

Ever notice we are happier when we are walking in tune with the Lord? When we are resting right up there under His wings, we get our joy revitalized.

*Because thou hast been my help, therefore in the shadow of thy wings will I rejoice. Psalm 63: 7*

## Final Thoughts

If you are a mother, that picture of a hen loving and protecting its chicks under its wings is such a powerful example. All those things we find under those wings are things we should strive to give our own children.

There is closeness, protection, comfort, trust, love, satisfaction, and rejoicing.

I'm so glad that I have a God who cares so much about me that He keeps me up *under His wings.* I know there are times that I get like David running from Saul and need to go sliding under those feathers and into that safe place.

And boy, sometimes I feel like I just get too many boo-boos to count and I long for that comfort that only God can give. There have been times when I've been so sad that I can't even speak to the Lord when I get up under there, but I know He understands and He makes me feel better.

I love benefiting from all those things I find when I get up under those wings. All those things I find there only makes me stronger so that I can grow in the Lord.

**So, what are you finding under His wings?**

# 5

# FLOWER LANGUAGE

*Whoso keepeth his mouth and his tongue keepeth*
*his soul from troubles.  Proverbs 21:23*

**R**ecently I was thinking about snapdragon flowers and it occurred to me that I can get a little "snappy" myself sometimes.  Perhaps maybe act like a dragon too.  It brought to my mind some other flower language I may not want to speak as well.  Be assured that I do love these type of flowers, but I figure they can teach me a few lessons as well as being pretty.

## Snapdragon

We usually think about dragons leaving a trail of destruction behind them.  What about you?  Is your mouth and tongue prone to snap?  Snapping with our mouth can leave a lot of destruction wherever we go. Singe anyone's hair lately?  Leaving puffs of smoke in your wake?

*A soft answer turneth away wrath: but grievous*
*words stir up anger.  Proverbs 15:1*

## Tulips

When we say someone has "two lips" we mean that they have a tendency to speak out of two sides of their mouth.  Do you speak one way about a subject to one person and another way about that subject to another?  Do you speak with flattering lips?

*Put away from thee a froward mouth, and perverse*
*lips put far from thee.  Proverbs 4:24*

*They speak vanity every one with his neighbour:*
*with flattering lips and with a double heart do*
*they speak.  Psalm 12:2*

## Bachelor's Buttons

I think we all have trouble with this one.  There are just so many times when we should just keep our lips buttoned, but frankly it can be hard to do.  Sometimes we could avoid so much trouble if we would just have kept our mouths shut.

If we don't keep our lips buttoned, we'll be a *"bachelor"* in theory as no one will want to be around us.

*In the multitude of words there wanteth not sin: but he that refraineth his lips is wise. Proverbs 10:19*

*A talebearer revealeth secrets: but he that is of a faithful spirit concealeth the matter. Proverbs 11:13*

## Red Hot Poker

Pokers are used to stir the embers around in the fireplace but some of us have a habit of doing the same thing with our tongues. We can't leave well enough alone. We have to stir up trouble with our words.

Do you have any ashes and embers left on your tongue?

*And withal they learn to be idle, wandering about from house to house; and not only idle, but tattlers also and busybodies, speaking things which they ought not. 1 Timothy 5:13*

*A froward man soweth strife: and a whisperer separateth chief friends.  Proverbs 16:28*

## Dracula

Did you know there was such a thing as a dracula flower?  Some of us have dracula mouths.  We go sinking our teeth in and just sucking the blood right out of others by what we say.  We give those little digs into people with words.  Have you left your teeth marks on anyone lately?

*He that hateth dissembleth with his lips, and layeth up deceit within him.  Proverbs 26:24*

*To speak evil of no man, to be no brawlers, but gentle, shewing all meekness unto all men.  Titus 3:2*

## Scorpion Orchids

Scorpions have stingers which can be very venomous and also they have those claws that clench.  Do you sting with your tongue?  Grasp ahold of your victim and squeeze with what you say?  Is your tongue dangerous?  Some scorpions aren't very harmful but some have stings that can become fatal.

How venomous are you? How long do you leave the victim of your speech burning with pain?

*They have sharpened their tongues like a serpent;*
*adders' poison is under their lips. Selah. Psalm 140:3*

## Elephant Ears

This one is not really a flower, but a plant. We can learn from it too though because what we do with our ears has an effect on our speech.

Got big ears? Some of us just are waiting and listening for some gossip to come floating to our ears.

Are you looking forward to hearing what you can about somebody or anybody? Do you go looking for what dirt you can dig up on people and perhaps repeat it?

*The words of a talebearer are as wounds, and they go*
*down into the innermost parts of the belly. Proverbs 26:22*

*Let no corrupt communication proceed out of your mouth,*

*but that which is good to the use of edifying, that it may minister grace unto the hearers. Ephesians 4:29*

## Dandelion

These as most of you know are not flowers but really weeds. Weeds that spread. They do look pretty though and I suppose all of us have picked them when we were kids just as if they were real flowers.

Ever blow on a dandelion puff? You know, that white head that has the seeds all over it? I'm not sure if there is a scientific name for it other than "dandelion puff". They go everywhere in the wind. Don't they?

Lying is kind of like a dandelion. When you start lying, it spreads like weeds. Lies will just keep popping out of your mouth unless you get it under control.

*Lying lips are abomination to the LORD: but they that deal truly are his delight. Proverbs 12:22*

*A lying tongue hateth those that are afflicted by it; and a flattering mouth worketh ruin. Proverbs 26:28*

## <u>Final Thoughts</u>

There are so many things about our speech that we need to tend to and care for or we may find ourselves with things growing there that don't make us proud.

Our speech garden needs to be nurtured and tended to properly so that it doesn't get out of control. Perhaps fertilize some so that good speech grows, weed out the bad speech and negative comments, and clip the vines on those things that come flying out of our mouths that aren't edifying before they wind their way around and strangle those we come in contact with.

From now on, I think when someone says a person speaks with "flowery words", I'll have to think twice about that.

## So, what's growing in your flower garden?

# 6

## LADYBUG! LADYBUG!

*What? know ye not that your body is the temple of the*
*Holy Ghost which is in you, which ye have of God,*
*and ye are not your own? 1 Corinthians 6: 19*

Ladybugs are unique creatures. I don't really like bugs in general so ladybugs are about the only bug I like. I guess because they are so bright and cute, even if they are beetles. I can remember when I was little I would catch ladybugs and let them crawl across my fingers.

I think it is interesting that scientists tell the different species of ladybugs apart by the number of spots they have.

I wonder if people can tell us by our spots? We are ladies of God. Do we show that fact by how we conduct ourselves? Are we talking, walking, sitting, dressing, acting, and thinking like godly ladies?

**Talk like a lady.**

There is nothing appealing about foul and filthy

language coming out of a woman's mouth. It's even less appealing when it comes out of a Christian woman.

It is not just foul language that can get us into trouble though. Let's not forget the other things that come out of our mouths too. Unkind words, harsh comments, nagging, gossiping, and complaining are some. Those are things that don't add up to godly *spots*.

> *She openeth her mouth with wisdom; and in her tongue is the law of kindness. Proverbs 31:26*

> *Let no corrupt communication proceed out of your mouth, but that which is good to the use of edifying, that it may minister grace unto the hearers. Ephesians 4:29*

## Walk like a lady.

When I was in high school, I had a charm class and I remember the teacher having us walk with a book on our head. I recall her telling us not to gallop like horses and not to walk like we just got off of one. That is good advice. An even gait is much more pleasing.

How do you walk? It's probably something you don't think about. Do you clomp your shoes, barrel over people, or even trot like that horse?

We don't want to forget about our spiritual walk as well. Seeking the Lord daily in prayer and Bible study will help us walk more like Christ wants us to walk.

*And walk in love, as Christ also hath loved us, and hath given himself for us an offering and a sacrifice to God for a sweet smelling savour. Ephesians 5:2*

## Sit like a lady.

I was told over and over when I was young to sit like a lady and I find myself telling my daughters the same thing. Sitting like a lady is important. When you don't sit like a lady it can send all the wrong signals and it isn't pleasing to those around you either.

How we sit spiritually speaking is important too. The Bible tells us to be careful in this area. Over in Psalm 1:1 it talks about sitting "in the seat of the scornful" (those that reject and mock Christ for who He is).

> *Blessed is the man that walketh not in the counsel of the ungodly, nor standeth in the way of sinners, nor sitteth in the seat of the scornful. Psalm 1:1*

Where do you find yourself sitting? Is it with bad company? Maybe you have a problem with sitting and being idle. Maybe you have the problem with too much sitting in front of the TV or computer. Maybe you spend too much time sitting and gossiping.

Proverbs 31:27 talks about how the Proverbs 31 lady "eateth not the bread of idleness." How you sit will show your spots.

## Dress like a lady.

What you wear will show your spots too. Have you ever noticed that verse in Proverbs 7:10?

> *And, behold, there met him a woman with the attire of an harlot, and subtil of heart. Proverbs 7:10*

The woman in this verse was associated with the clothes that she wore just like we are. Some people think it doesn't matter what you wear because people should look on the heart and not your clothes. Face it. Only God looks at the heart. Man is always going to look at the outward appearance.

I'm not saying you get so caught up in your appearance that you go overboard, but we are to be careful in this area. You don't want to hinder the cause of Christ by what you wear.

*In like manner also, that women adorn*
*themselves in modest apparel... 1 Timothy 2:9*

Modesty is not the only thing important where the area of dress is concerned. Some of us have the modesty part under control. We'd never think of wearing something too tight, too low, too short, etc. But in the areas of sloppiness and unkempt appearances we can sometimes be a little lacking.

When you are wearing clothes three sizes too big, stained up clothes, wrinkled clothes, or clothing that just doesn't fit in general, it isn't giving a good impression. I think this is an area that needs more attention, not just the modesty aspect, but dressing like ladies in a clean and neat fashion.

We ought to be pleasing the Lord in how we dress. I don't think He's pleased by sloppiness on our part. We're His and our body is His. I find myself falling into the sloppiness trap because I like to be comfortable, but we are children of the King and we should dress our best. I know this is something I really need to work on.

*What? know ye not that your body is the temple of the Holy Ghost which is in you, which ye have of God, and ye are not your own? 1 Corinthians 6:19*

## Act like a lady.

How we act will definitely show our spots. Have you ever stopped to consider how you act when you are around other people? Are you loud, boisterous, pushy, and unkind? Or, are you considerate and even-tempered? How do you act towards your family and to your husband?

Did you know that the ladybug goes through a

complete metamorphosis?  We as Christian women should be changed in Christ.  We need to put off the *"old man"* and put on Christ.

*That ye put off concerning the former conversation*
*the old man, which is corrupt according to the*
*deceitful lusts. Ephesians 4:22*

The ladybug uses its antennae to touch, smell and taste.  We have our own antennae in the Word of God.  We should let it be our guide when it comes to what we allow ourselves to be involved in as Christian ladies.

Another fact about ladybugs is that they are helpful.  They continuously eat all those bad things like aphids (plant lice), potato beetles and corn bores.  Ladybugs are considered to be the most beneficial of all insects.  How beneficial are we?  Are we helpful godly ladies?

**Think like a lady.**

If we are not thinking  like a lady, it's going  to be harder for us to talk, walk, sit, dress, and act like one. We have to keep our hearts and minds focused on Christ in order to be the godly lady we should. Where have your thoughts been lately? Are you focusing on things that a godly lady should?

*Casting down imaginations, and every high thing that exalteth itself against the knowledge of God, and bringing into captivity every thought to the obedience of Christ. 2 Corinthians 10:5*

*Finally, brethren, whatsoever things are true, whatsoever things are honest, whatsoever things are just, whatsoever things are pure, whatsoever things are lovely, whatsoever things are of good report; if there be any virtue, and if there be any praise, think on these things. Philippians 4:8*

## Final Thoughts

One of the dictionary definitions of a "lady" is "a woman of high social position" and the second part of that definition is "a woman who is polite, well-mannered and refined".

As Christian women we do have a "high social position". This isn't on a worldly level, but if we are born again Christians, we are children of the King. We are part of a royal family and we should act accordingly.

Being "polite" and "well-mannered" should come in tow. When we allow Christ to take over our lives, our thinking, actions, speech, and behavior will reflect Him and we'll become those godly ladies that we should.

**So, are you conducting yourself like a lady?**

# 7

# "SON" FLOWERS

*For the LORD God is a sun and shield: the LORD will give grace and glory: no good thing will he withhold from them that walk uprightly. Psalm 84:11*

Sunflowers are so pretty. I love the yellow and gold tones in their coloring, but they also stand so tall and majestic looking too. I can remember when I was little, my dad would sometimes plant them along the garden so they conjure up good memories for me as well.

Sunflowers are one of those things you see everywhere such as on dishes, tablecloths, pillows, and other things for the home. They are right up there with roses when it comes to popularity.

Did you know that even Picasso and Van Gogh painted sunflowers? Probably because they are such a beautiful and distinctive flower.

I have studied the sunflower a little bit and have learned five lessons from them. Come with me as we discuss each of those five things.

## Sunflowers track the sun.

Most plants are attracted to light but the flowering head of the sunflower actually tracks the sun, following its path and moving toward where it is in the sky all during the day.

I read somewhere that sunflowers track the sun when they are in bud stage. Isn't that how it usually goes for us as Christians? When we first come to know the Lord, we get excited about knowing all about Him and living for Him, but after a while we sometimes grow a little preoccupied with other things and get our eyes off of the Lord.

Wouldn't it be great if as a Christian we'd track the Son of God and follow Him all day long? No matter what was going on in our lives and throughout our day, we wouldn't take our eyes off of the Son?

## Sunflowers need to be stabilized.

The second thing I've learned about the sunflower is that it that it needs to be firmly planted in the soil in order to grow. Sunflowers grow so tall and their stems become so heavy that they will topple over if they aren't stabilized in the ground.

I know as a Christian it's very easy to topple over if we are not grounded in the Word of God. We need to know what and why we believe what we do so our feet are firmly planted and we won't falter in our Christian growth.

**Sunflowers produce seeds.**

Did you know that a single sunflower can have up to 2,000 seeds? When we think about sowing seeds as a Christian, just think of the potential reach that each of us can have to spread the Gospel. It could be limitless if we would just sow those seeds.

**Sunflowers produce oil.**

The oil that the sunflower produces is considered a good oil with healthy benefits. As Christians we should be producing the fruit of the spirit (love, joy, peace, longsuffering, gentleness, goodness, faith, meekness, temperance).

All of those have some healthy benefits on us as

Christians and on others that we meet.

## Sunflowers resemble the sun.

Sunflowers not only follow the sun but when you look at them, they resemble the sun too. Resembling the Son should be one of those things we do as a Christian. Being Christ-like is an essential part of being a Christian.

## Final Thoughts

When I think about the lessons from the sunflower, my mind goes to that fifth chapter of Ephesians where it's talking about following God and all the ways we are to act as Christians. It starts out in the first couple verses by saying,

> *Be ye therefore followers of God, as dear children;*
> *And walk in love, as Christ also hath loved us, and*
> *hath given himself for us an offering and a sacrifice*
> *to God for a sweetsmelling savour. Ephesians 5:1-2*

The chapter goes on in detail on various topics of Christian living and mentions all those bad things we are to avoid, starting with "fornication" and it goes on from there. In verses 15-16 it says,

*See then that ye walk circumspectly, not as fools, but as wise, Redeeming the time, because the days are evil.*

I am not going to type the entire chapter out here but I think that whole chapter is so important as guidance to our everyday Christian lives. It shows us what getting up and following the Son all day and being a SON flower is all about.

It boils down to walking in the Spirit, following God, and living Christ-like as a Christian should. We've got to live that way in order to "redeem the time" and spread the Gospel of Christ.

## So, are you living like a SON-flower?

# 8

## EYES WIDE OPEN

*Mine eyes are ever toward the LORD... Psalm 25:15*

It is finally warming up around here and I've been noticing all the little bugs and insects around. There are bees and wasps where I park every day and wait for my daughter to get out of school.

They want so badly to come inside my car. I roll the windows down because I'm hot. Then I roll them up to keep the bees or wasps out. It depends which one is bugging me that day.

I repeat that up and down with the windows several times in just the space of a few minutes (as I get panicky that they might get me).

All those insects are a little *buggy* at times but I sure enjoy watching all those little critters that are God's creation.

I was thinking about all these small things and the dragonfly came to mind. Now it is one of those mysterious creatures that God created. Dragonflies have those big eyes wide open.

I've read that their sight encompasses basically 360 degrees and that they can see everything at most angles. Wish I could see like that, especially those things that seem to sneak up on me and sideswipe me.

There are things I wish I could have seen coming. I know there are things that as Christians we should watch out for so we don't get off track in our daily living. We need to have our eyes wide open like a dragonfly.

## We need eyes wide open to understanding.

If we would keep our eyes open to understanding the Lord, just think how much better we would get to know Him.

Look what it says about the eyes of our understanding in Ephesians.

*The eyes of your understanding being enlightened;*
*that ye may know what is the hope of his calling,*
*and what the riches of the glory of his inheritance*
*in the saints. Ephesians 1:18*

## We need eyes wide open to the Word.

I guess if we had our eyes wide open to what God's Word says, we'd learn more and be better to handle those things that get into our view.

*Mine eyes prevent the night watches, that I might meditate in thy word.  Psalm 119:148*

*Open thou mine eyes, that I may behold  wondrous things out of thy law.  Psalm 119:18*

## We need eyes wide open to temptation.

Just think how much smoother our lives would be if we were constantly on guard for this one.  We know we are supposed to be on our toes for it because it will come sneaking in and be right there in front of us before we see it.

*Watch and pray, that ye enter not into temptation... Matthew 26:41*

## We need eyes wide open to God's help.

We get into these situations and our eyes bug out because here  comes trouble.  How much  better we could handle it if we constantly had our eyes on God and were really relying on the Lord.

*I will lift up mine eyes unto the hills, from*
*whence cometh my help.  Psalm 121:1*

## **Final Thoughts**

Without that 360 degree sight, dragonflies wouldn't be able to be ready to make the quick maneuvers that they need to make in midair.

I think that when we keep our eyes wide open to certain things, we are better able to maneuver too. We are better able to handle all those things that come sailing into our view.

All in all, I think we need to keep our eyes on the Lord because He is the One who sees all.  The Lord can see up ahead where we can't and that's a nice fact in which to rest.  He can see behind us where we may have missed something.  He can also help us handle those things that come whizzing past us.

### **So, are your eyes wide open?**

# 9

# SEEDS OF KINDNESS

*And be ye kind one to another, tenderhearted,*
*forgiving one another, even as God for Christ's*
*sake hat forgiven you. Ephesians 4:32*

As we take a look at kindness, we need to realize that it is something that comes from within that we manifest outward in what we say and what we do.

When we say that someone is kind, we don't usually mean they are kind to themselves but that they are kind to others. So what we see is that kindness involves our relationships.

Reflect for a minute on all the people that you have in your life--your spouse, your kids, your in-laws, your friends, strangers, anyone you come in contact with. How are your relationships with these people? If they were asked, would they say you are a kind person?

In today's society it is very easy to come across those who are not kind. If you haven't met many unkind people, you must not get out much!

Think about Christmas time. It should be the most loving time of year and yet sometimes that's when we seem to encounter all those unkind people that come out from under their unkind rocks.

Have you been to the grocery store or to a department store on a busy day? Next time while you're looking around or waiting in line at the counter, listen to all the conversations around you. More than likely you'll come across some unkind people speaking unkind words.

Christ wants us to be different. He doesn't want Christians to be crawling out from behind unkind rocks. We are not to be like those in this world but our words and actions should be a light to lost souls. Our verse says, "Be ye kind one to another..."

The next thing in the verse listed along with being kind is "tenderhearted". When we start being tenderhearted it is easy to be kind. We start looking at the world with new eyes which are full of compassion.

If our hearts are tender it means that they are easily touched and sensitive. If we are sensitive to those around us we start seeing their needs instead of our own. It in turn makes our actions toward them more kind. So, how do we begin sowing those seeds of kindness?

## Remember who you are.

If we want to work on being kind we need to first remember who we are.

*Put on therefore, as the elect of God, holy and beloved, bowels of mercies, kindness, humbleness of mind, meekness, longsuffering. Colossians 3:12*

It refers to us as "the elect of God". We are God's children. The verse lists "kindness" right there along with the other things that we should manifest as a Christian. If we don't have kindness, how will we ever convince others that the Christian life is worth living? Also, how can we show love to other Christians except through our deeds of kindness?

## Follow Christ's example.

To develop those seeds of kindness that we need

to sow in our lives we must look to Christ. He is our ultimate example.

*How God anointed Jesus of Nazareth with the Holy*
*Ghost and with power: who went about doing good,*
*and healing all that were oppressed of the devil;*
*for God was with him. Acts 10:38*

Jesus *"went about doing good"*. Following Christ is a big part of the Christian life. We as Christians want to follow His example in certain areas of our life such as in our prayer life and witnessing, but we forget sometimes about all the good deeds Christ portrayed.

Just because we don't get to heaven by our good works, we sometimes push aside any idea of any good works altogether. Christ said,

*By this shall all men know that ye are my disciples,*
*if ye have love one to another. John 13:35*

How can we show our love without being kind and doing good deeds? Wouldn't that be a great epitaph to have on our grave? "He (or she) went about doing good."

## Develop compassion.

When Christ looked on the crowds He had compassion on them. The Bible says that He "was moved with compassion" Matthew 9:36.

Christ could see each hurting soul and He genuinely cared about them. Our Lord showed His compassion with His actions. When we develop compassion in our lives we can't help but show it through the seeds of kindness that we begin to sow.

Have you read the parable of the Good Samaritan lately? The Good Samaritan went out of his way to help the wounded man. Have we gone out of our way to show compassion for someone?

## Begin one kind deed at a time.

Look around you. Who could use a simple act of kindness? There are hurting people all about us. Maybe you know someone who is just lonely. If you aren't in the habit of sowing seeds of kindness, start with something simple.

How about a smile and a kind word to someone? Send a note of encouragement to someone who is going through a hard time. Anything nice you do for someone can be considered an act of kindness.

Determine to do at least one kind thing a week and pretty soon it will come naturally to you.

*As we have therefore opportunity, let us do good unto all men, especially unto them who are of the household of faith. Galatians 6:10*

## Final Thoughts

If we are ever going to make an impact on the world as Christians, we are going to have to start being more kind. We are going to have to remember who we are in Christ and how we act. Just increasing how many seeds we sow little by little can have a huge impact on the world.

**So, are you sowing seeds of kindness?**

# 10

# BUZZIN' ALONG!

*For where your treasure is, there will
your heart be also. Matthew 6: 21*

**S**ometimes I enjoy watching the bees buzzing along in our backyard. That is, as long as they don't get too close to me. They never stay long in one spot. They just hover here and there keeping busy with their job of pollination.

When I consider the bees, I wonder what I am *buzzin'* along doing? I think of the Proverbs 31 woman and how she buzzed around.

*"She...worketh willingly with her hands." (vs. 13)*
*"She riseth also while it is yet night" (vs. 15)*
*"She layeth her hands to the spindle" (vs. 19)*
*"She stretcheth out her hand to the poor." (vs. 20)*
*"She maketh fine linen, and selleth it" (vs. 24)*
*"She looketh well to the ways of her household" (vs. 27)*

There is nothing wrong with being busy. The

Proverbs 31 woman demonstrates this. It also shows that she was accomplishing much.

I wonder how much I accomplish? I don't want to just be *buzzin'* along just to buzz and not accomplishing anything. Sometimes I think I'm guilty of that.

I think it's a trap we can all easily fall into by putting too much on our plates. I think we all need to slow down from time to time and really evaluate what it is we are buzzing about. We may need to ask ourselves some questions.

## What am I busy doing?

You may need to just list out your daily routine to actually see what you are doing. Are there things that you could cut out? Are there things you need to add?

Maybe you need to make a calendar and get organized. The bees could never accomplish all they need to do without order. Sometimes it is good to just plan everything out on a calendar and see what we have going on in our lives.

## What are my priorities?

You may need to take a look at the things that play an importance in your life and evaluate whether they should be a priority. Are they taking away from your family time or time in God's Word? Maybe make a list of what's really important to you.

## Am I accomplishing anything for Christ?

With all of your *buzzin'*, are you making your life count for the Lord? Looking back to Matthew 6:21, where is your treasure?

> *For where your treasure is, there*
> *will your heart be also.*

## <u>Final Thoughts</u>

Sometimes we all need to get a perspective on the things that we are buzzing along doing in our lives. We need to live in motion, but we need to be careful that we don't become overwhelmed too. There are times we need to slow down and reflect on the Lord.

> *Be still, and know that I am God... Psalm 46:10*

We've got to get our priorities set so that we can enjoy our lives and our families. Sometimes we have to stop and see what we are *buzzin'* about and get our buzzing going in the right direction in order to live life to the fullest.

**So, what are you *buzzin'* along doing?**

# 11

# FRAGRANCE OF BEAUTY

*And walk in love, as Christ also hath loved us, and*
*hath given himself for us an offering and a sacrifice*
*to God for a sweetsmelling savour. Ephesians 5:2*

There is just something about roses. They have been a favorite throughout time. We must want them in our homes because they're manufactured on everything from furniture to bed linens. Lovers send them and many songs have been written about them.

Why do we love roses so much? Perhaps because they are so beautiful, but I think it is more than that. They are not only beautiful but they also smell so wonderful. Beauty with fragrance. What a combination!

Have you ever thought that's probably a great combination for a Christian woman to have? It would be great if not only when people saw us, they'd realize we are a Christian, but after they've gotten close to us and been around us, they'd think, *Wow! They smell like a Christian too.*

I'm afraid some of us don't have a pleasing smell all the time. It's not anything physical. Most of us are sure to wash and slap on our deodorant as we go on our way. It's just plain and simple. Most of us don't want to stink. It's not acceptable to walk down the street and not have a pleasing body odor.

So why do we think it is acceptable to be a Christian that doesn't have a pleasant smell? Sometimes our thinking is that it is okay to stink as a Christian. We think to ourselves that our attitude is just a little off so it won't matter much. Or we think we'll just keep this one bad habit in our lives. It shouldn't make me smell too offensive. Should it?

We will hurl harsh words at someone and walk away without a thought of the fragrance that it will leave in the air.

Ever notice that most people with body odor don't even know they have it? They have not taken care of their cleanliness in so long that they don't even know they are offending others.

It is the same way with us as Christians. We start letting our attitudes slide, our time with God dwindle down, and pretty soon we're not leaving a pleasant scent on the world. The sad thing is that we've gotten used to the smell and we don't even know it's there.

There comes a time when we need to sniff under our spiritual arms and say, *do I stink?* We need to get back on track to being sweet smelling women for the Lord. We need to strive to be the fragrant roses God intended us to be.

Let's cultivate ourselves to improve our fragrance.

**Be kind.**

Nothing smells up a place more than someone who isn't kind. It's totally opposite of what we're instructed to do.

*And be ye kind one to another... Ephesians 4:32*

*Charity suffereth long, and is kind... 1 Corinthians 13:4*

## Be forgiving.

How can we be sending off a fragrant odor if we hold grudges and never forgive those whom we know we should forgive?

> *...forgiving one another, even as God for Christ's sake hath forgiven you. Ephesians 4:32*

## Be joyful.

No one wants to be around a miserable person. When you aren't happy in the Lord, you rub off on other people. In other words, your bad smell spreads. Find joy in the Lord. Study His Word and have time in prayer to fellowship with Him.

> *And my soul shall be joyful in the LORD: it shall rejoice in his salvation. Psalm 35:9*

## Be content.

What an odor someone who's not content can put off. Grumbling and the self-pity parties usually come in tow. It isn't very refreshing to be around a discontented person.

*Not that I speak in respect of want: for I have learned, in whatsoever state I am, therewith to be content.  Philippians 4:11*

## **Final Thoughts**

We can either choose to be a breath of fresh air or we can choose to dampen the spirits of those we come in contact with.  Living our lives to please and honor the Lord is important.

A Christian without a pleasing fragrance won't accomplish much for the Lord.  We've got to try to be more like Him, the 'Rose' of Sharon.  We need to live our lives in a way where the love of Christ flows through us and causes us to be a sweet smelling aroma on the world.

**So, what kind of fragrance did you leave as you walked today?**

# 12

# TAKE IT SLOW

*Wherefore, my beloved brethren, let every man be swift
to hear, slow to speak, slow to wrath. James 1:19*

Have you ever thought about the things in life
that take it slow? There is the turtle, slug, and snail
of course. They don't move very fast.

You have probably all had someone tell you to
"take it slow" or you have told someone else that. It
is probably the one thing we say when we teach our
kids how to ride a bike or even to drive a car.

There are all kinds of situations when we say,
"take it slow".

Why do we say that phrase to people? Well,
usually because we want that person to either be
safe, do well at something, perhaps not injure
others, get the most out of something, endure to the
end, and so on.

The Lord tells us to be slow about a couple things
in the Bible too.

## Take it slow in our speech.

We have to slow down and think before we speak. When we speak first before thinking or before knowing the whole situation, we can get into trouble. Look up the following verses to help you get a handle on your speech.

*Proverbs 29:20*      *Ecclesiastes 5:2*
*Proverbs 15:28*      *Proverbs 18:13*

## Take it slow before we get angry.

Anger can be explosive. It can lead to a lot of fighting and bickering, hurt people, and hurt our witness for Christ. Proverbs 29:22 says,

*An angry man stirreth up strife...*

We have to learn to control ourselves where our anger is concerned. Look up the following verses to help you get a handle on anger.

*Ecclesiastes 7:9*      *Proverbs 14:29*
*Proverbs 15:18*      *Proverbs 16:32*

## <u>Final Thoughts</u>

The Lord tells us these things about taking it slow for our benefit. He is trying to help us avoid so many mistakes. He may want us to avoid getting hurt ourselves or avoid our actions hurting others.

When the Lord tells us to "take it slow", He wants the best for us.

## So, are you taking it slow?

# 13

# DON'T STEP ON THAT ANT!

*Go to the ant, thou sluggard; consider her*
*ways, and be wise. Proverbs 6:6*

## Dig Deeper:  Read Proverbs 6:1-11

We shouldn't step on that ant, at least till we learn from it.  I always love all the lessons that the world around us can teach us.  It always amazes me how tiny and insignificant we think these things are and yet we can really learn some valuable lessons from them if we just study them a little bit.

That is what it is saying in Proverbs 6.  Study that ant.  Consider how it works.  Consider how it lives.

Verse 6 is directed to the "sluggard".  That is another way to say, "lazy".  If we look in the verses above this in Proverbs 6 (verses 1-5), we see that it is talking about someone who has basically taken on the debt of another person.

It is kind of like we would think of as co-signing a

loan these days. It isn't a wise thing to do today and it wasn't a wise thing to do back in Solomon's day.

He tells the man to "deliver thyself" (verse 3). In other words, get out of it. Not only that but he tells him in that same verse to do it quickly. "Do it now". Don't delay. Get it done. Get it done even before you sleep.

Look at verse 4.

*Give not sleep to thine eyes, nor slumber to thine eyelids.*

I love reading through Proverbs. I notice so many times how the things in it are said with urgency, like in this passage. Solomon, full of wisdom, is giving out warnings and trying to get our attention that there is an imperative nature to things.

When they are left unattended, there can be serious consequences. He says here in this passage that it is important that this get done right away. Then he admonishes the sluggard to go to the ant and learn from it.

The ants are anything but lazy. They work hard and they work together to get things done.

*Which having no guide, overseer, or ruler, Provideth her meat in the summer, and gathereth her food in the harvest. Proverbs 6:7-8*

## Ants take the initiative.

The first thing I notice here is that ants have initiative. They don't have anyone who is over them to tell them what to do or how to act or how to work. They have "no guide, overseer, or ruler".

I wish my kids had the initiative to empty the dishwasher or to take out the trash without being told. I sure have to be the overseer in my house to make sure chores are done.

Ants on the other hand just do what needs to be done. They just do it.

## Ants plan in advance.

The next thing I see here is that ants are planners. They don't wait until the last minute to get things done. They plan. They prepare. The ant "provideth her meat in the summer, and gathereth her food in the harvest."

They don't have to worry about their food in the winter because they have gathered it and preserved it already. Those ants have their food all lined on their pantry shelves and ready to eat when they need it.

I would like to be a little more like the ants in this area. Planning in advance can really keep things running smoothly and efficiently.

## Ants work as a team.

If we look over in Proverbs 30, we see where again, we are to take notice of the ant.

*There be four things which are little upon the earth, but they are exceeding wise: The ants are a people not strong, yet they prepare their meat in the summer; Proverbs 30:24-25*

Notice it says, that ants are "not strong". They are tiny little creatures. One little ant can be squashed by just about anything. We are used to calling ants *problems* though, and do you know why that is? They work as a team.

We can all handle one ant in our home but when they are working together to march their little legs all over, they become a big problem.

If you have ever read or know much about ants, they do everything as a team. They each have their jobs. Some take care of baby ants. Some gather food. Some dig. Some fight for protection. Those ants have smooth operations running in those anthills.

Each ant knows its role and does it. They work together for the good of each other and for their survival. They all have the same goal.

We have the same goal as Christians too. That is to spread the Gospel. We've got to start working as a team to get it done and we can't be lazy about it.

## **Final Thoughts**

I hope I can learn more from the ant. I'd like to be wise in the end. I'd like to take the initiative more, especially when it comes to witnessing for the Lord. I need to just step out and do it.

Planning in advance is a trait I'd like to have more of too. I know I definitely need to work on that. I don't want to go through life with *folded hands* and find out the consequences in the end.

*How long wilt thou sleep, O sluggard? when wilt thou arise out of thy sleep? Yet a little sleep, a little slumber, a little folding of the hands to sleep: So shall thy poverty come as one that travelleth, and thy want as an armed man. Proverbs 6:9-11*

It boggles my mind to think of all the work those little ants do. They travel so far and carry so much. It makes me wonder how much I really do when it comes to preparing for the future where eternity is concerned.

How far am I willing to go for the Lord? Am I working as diligently as I should? I know I have to be "always abounding" as it says in 1 Corinthians.

*Therefore, my beloved brethren, be ye stedfast, unmoveable, always abounding in the work of the Lord, forasmuch as ye know that your labour is not in vain in the Lord. 1 Corinthians 15:58*

# Remember what Jesus said?

*I must work the works of him that sent me,*
*while it is day: the night cometh, when no*
*man can work.  John 9:4*

## So, have you considered the ant lately?

# 14

# HAVING THAT OLD TREE AGE

*But grow in grace, and in the knowledge of our Lord*
*and Saviour Jesus Christ. To him be glory both now*
*and for ever. Amen. 2 Peter 3:18*

Do you remember studying about the layers of trees when you were younger and in school? Each layer inside the tree forms a recognizable ring. Those rings the layers make in the tree are how we determine the age of the tree.

Scientists study these rings to reconstruct the history of the tree. They can determine the climate the tree grew in because they can see by the width of the rings how wet or dry the years were.

They can tell how much air pollution affected the tree. They can even study the migration of insects through tree rings. The size and shape of the rings can also tell how much sunlight the tree absorbed.

I wonder how many layers I have as a Christian and what kind of story I tell? If someone could look inside and see my layers as a Christian, what would they see?

Did I allow the "Son" light to shine on me and did I drink in the water of the Word of God adequately? Am I a mature Christian?

Here are some layers of trees to think about.

## Outer Bark

This is the tree's protection from the outside world. What about me? How do I protect myself as a Christian? Am I using that armor that it talks about in Ephesians 6? I know I need to build up that wall of prayer and trust in God to be protected by what the elements of the world may rain down on me.

## Phloem

This is the inner bark of the tree. It is the pipeline from which the inner tree receives food from the leaves and outside of the tree. In order for a Christian to grow, we need to be taking in God's Word and all that it offers us as Christians. Without food, nothing will grow. We need that pipeline!

## Cambium

This is the cell layer of the tree. It is the growing part. This is the one layer of a tree that is considered alive. It annually produces new bark and wood. It's what makes the bark, branches, and roots grow thicker.

I wonder how I do that as a Christian? I think the need here is that I remain active for Christ. I need to keep keeping on by staying in the Word, witnessing, and doing all I can to show the love of Christ to others. I need to be alive in Christ to grow taller and sturdier as a Christian.

## Xylem or Sapwood

This layer moves the water up through the leaves to give the tree the water it needs. This reminds me of what the Holy Spirit can do when we allow Him to work through us.

## Heartwood

This is the center part of the tree. Although it is the dead part of the tree, it won't fall apart as long as the other layers are intact. This part of the tree actually becomes firm.

That's kind of like us as a Christian, we won't fall apart if we have our layers in place. We need to be doing all those things like growing, taking in God's Word, and allowing the Holy Spirit to work in us. Having that firm foundation in Christ will help us to be supported and stand for the long term.

## Final Thoughts

Frankly, as Christians, we should be acting our age. As we grow in our Christian life there are things that we should be better able to handle because we are spiritually mature.

There are things we may not deal with well as saplings but as we get older in Christ, we should be able to deal with them differently such as when we are faced with anger, fear, criticism, worry, and bitterness.

We should always be adding those layers to our Christian life that will help us better withstand the world. We need to build up layers of faith. We need obedience, love, and all those Christian traits.

Those layers will make us strong like a towering tree. When we are strong in Christ we should be able to withstand some of the things we couldn't before. When the wind and elements of the world come swirling by we should be able to stand tall.

God wants us to grow. He wants us to put aside those things that don't pertain to us as Christians and move on with growing in Him.

*Wherefore laying aside all malice, and all guile, and hypocrisies, and envies, and all evil speakings, As newborn babes, desire the sincere milk of the word, that ye may grow thereby: If so be ye have tasted that the Lord is gracious. 1 Peter 2:1-3*

On over in 2 Peter it talks about the things we need to do in order to grow as a Christian. The writer urges us not to be led away by the world, but to stand steadfast in what we believe.

*Ye therefore, beloved, seeing ye know these things before, beware lest ye also, being led away with the error of the wicked, fall from your own stedfastness.*

*But grow in grace, and in the knowledge of our Lord
and Saviour Jesus Christ. To him be glory both now
and for ever. Amen. 2 Peter 3:17,18*


None of us should stay baby Christians. We should want to grow up. I hope I have grown as a Christian over the years. I want my roots to go deep so that I can stand firm and be a mature Christian.

## So, is your age showing?

## 15

# GRAB YOUR FLY SWATTER!

*Whether therefore ye eat, or drink, or whatsoever*
*ye do, do all to the glory of God.   I Corinthians 10:31*

Have you ever considered the fly?  It's such a
small little thing and yet it can be so annoying and
can really get in your way just like a bad habit.
Think about how a fly buzzes around.

Have you ever sat and tried to relax and read a
book and there was a fly in the house?  Of all the
places to fly around, where does it go?  That's right.
Right on you, landing repeatedly on your hand.

You continually swat at it. Then it moves on to
your leg. You swat at it several times.  It goes away
for a few minutes and then before you know it back
it comes!

This time it lands on your ear.  You swat at it
again.  It buzzes around the room some more
checking out the curtains and windows and you
start to really get into your book and then buzz buzz,

it's right in your face this time.

That fly keeps pestering you over and over and you keep swatting at it with your hand, but it continually comes back to land on your skin! That fly will never go away by you swinging at it.

You have to finally go get the fly swatter. You have to have the right tool to take care of it and you have to actively pursue it to rid yourself of it. Swat! Finally it's taken care of.

It is the same way with a bad unspiritual habit that comes buzzing around in our lives. We know it's there and it keeps landing on us but somehow we find ourselves just swatting at it and never really taking care of the problem.

The only way to get rid of our bad habits is to get up and get the fly swatter or the right tool. Our best tool against bad habits is the Word of God. It is the best swatter for bad habits that you will ever find.

*All scripture is given by inspiration of God,*
*and is profitable for doctrine, for reproof, for*
*correction, for instruction in righteousness:*
*2 Timothy 3:16*

God's Word is actually so much better than a fly swatter. It acts like a heat seeking missile. *KABOOM!*

Take a minute to reflect on the fly that landed on you. Think about all the places that fly has been before it landed on your skin. Perhaps it was on that dead possum you passed along the road, in the smelly garbage can you opened this morning, buzzing on the backs of the pigs and cows that you passed in the fields along the road.

It's not pleasant to think about, but what do you end up with when there are flies around? You guessed it. Maggots! What does sin breed? Unspiritual habits!

The unspiritual bad habits we display in our lives are rooted in sin and sin has a way of smelling up our lives. I Corinthians 10:31. says "whatever ye do, do all to the glory of God."

If we are going to live this way we can't have bad habits hanging around buzzing to and fro. We have to take a good look at our lives, grab the right tool and actively pursue those things that keep us from honoring God.

## Getting Started

One of the best places to get started with our trustworthy swatter, God's Word, is by reading Colossians 3:1-17. If you want to improve your habits, start by seeking something better for yourself.

*If ye then be risen with Christ, seek those things which are above, where Christ sitteth on the right hand of God. Set your affection on things above, not on things on the earth.  Colossians 3:1-2*

## Things to Swat

You know exactly what bad habits you need to swat in your individual life, but Colossians 3 gives us some things to start with that can develop unspiritual habits.

In verse 5 it says to "mortify" our members concerning several things.  In other words, make these things dead in all parts of our body.  It's what we have to do in order to live that new life in Christ.

*fornication    uncleanness    inordinate affection*
*evil concupiscence    covetousness (idolatry)*

## More Things to Swat

As we go on in Colossians 3 to verses 8 and 9, we see more things that we are told to put off or that we can swat. These all can lead to unspiritual bad habits in our lives.

*Anger    wrath    malice    blasphemy*
*filthy communication    lies*

## Replacing Bad Habits

After we have asked for God's forgiveness for the bad habits which are rooted in sin, we need to commit not to get bogged down with them again.

*...seeing that ye have put off the old man with his deeds; And have put on the new man, which is renewed in knowledge after the image of him that created him. Colossians 3:9-10*

God helps us by giving us some things to replace the old things with in this same chapter of Colossians.

Here are just a few.

*bowels of mercies*    *kindness*    *humbleness*    *meekness*

Read on through verses 12-16 of that chapter to see what all we should be putting on and allowing in our lives as believers in Christ.

## Keeping Habits Under Control

If we are going to keep our habits under control then we are going to have to do as I Corinthians 10:31 says and do it all , "to the glory of God."

*And whatsoever ye do in word or deed, do all in the name of the Lord Jesus... Colossians 3:17*

## Final Thoughts

Getting a handle on our habits is an important thing in a Christian's life.   What we say and do should reflect our love for the Lord.

**So, are there things that you need to swat?**

# 16

# WIND POWER

*And grieve not the holy Spirit of God, whereby ye are*
*sealed unto the day of redemption. Ephesians 4:30*

**H**ave you ever watched a pinwheel move round and round? Most of us know that pinwheels don't just spin around on their own volition. There has to be a wind source of some kind.

You have to blow on it with your own breath or take it outside and allow the wind to move it. It won't spin around on its own strength.

That's just like us as Christians. We can't spin around on our own either. We need God's strength and power.

Of course, some of us try to spin around in our own strength anyway but we are not getting very far. Some of us have got some things stuck in our blades that are blocking our wind. Our power source is the Holy Spirit, and that is a powerful wind.

So much can be accomplished for Christ when we

allow the leading of the Holy Spirit in us. Just think about the disciples. They turned the world upside down.

We've all got things that get stuck in our blades and slow us down or even make our effectiveness for Christ come to a complete standstill. Here are some that came to my mind that are real power blockers.

## Bitterness

Whew! This one can really be a clog in your wheels. If you have bitterness in your life, you have to deal with it in order to have the power you need to keep spinning. Bitterness can rob you of your joy and eat away at you until you're not useful to anyone, let alone God.

*Let all bitterness...be put away from you.... Ephesians 4:31*

## Unforgiveness

If there is a rift between you and someone else and you don't deal with it, it's like running a rod right through your blades. You are not going to keep spinning with something like that stuck in your life. You'll find yourself not doing anything for Christ.

*And be ye kind one to another, tenderhearted, forgiving one another, even as God for Christ's sake hath forgiven you. Ephesians 4:32*

## Our Own Will

Trying to spin around all by ourselves and in our own direction isn't going to work. We have to give ourselves over to what God wants for us, which at times may not be exactly what we might want.

Living with our lives in tune with Christ daily is the only way we'll be sensitive to His will and not our own.

Look what it says for us to do in Romans 12.

*I beseech you therefore, brethren, by the mercies of God, that ye present your bodies a living sacrifice, holy, acceptable unto God, which is your reasonable service. And be not conformed to this world: but be ye transformed by the renewing of your mind, that ye may prove what is that good, and acceptable, and perfect, will of God. Romans 12:1-2*

## Unconfessed Sin

Of course if we have unconfessed sin in our lives, it's going to affect how the Holy Spirit works in us. We can't have something between God and us or there's not going to be any wind flow.

## **Final Thoughts**

If we are Christians, the Holy Spirit comes to reside in us. We have to be sensitive in order to allow His working. Do you have fruit in your life as a Christian? If not, you may not be allowing the power on your life that you need in order to keep spinning and serving Christ.

When my kids were little I would walk them to school from time to time and I remember one time in particular when we were down to one car and I walked the kids to school. They were in maybe kindergarten and first grade. My husband had taken the car to work so I had to walk the kids home from school.

It was on a hot day and my children were complaining. It *was* very hot, but as we began walking I could feel a slight breeze as we went under the first tree with branches that went out over the sidewalk where we were walking.

At the next tree I remember telling the kids to lift up their arms real high and feel the breeze. Ahhh. They thought that felt so good. So every tree along the way they'd stop and lift their arms up into the air.

They were so funny to watch. I'm sure all the passersby thought my kids were just a little bit weird, but they were feeling the effects of the wind going all through them and it was refreshing them. They kept saying, "Mom, come on! Lift up your arms too. It feels so good!"

I, of course was too embarrassed to walk down the street lifting my arms every little bit. It struck me then that that's how we Christians do. We keep our arms down and don't let the breeze of the Holy Spirit get to us even when we need to be refreshed.

We steel ourselves from being touched by a special song in church because we're too embarrassed to shed a few tears or we go into defense mode at invitation time because we don't want to go forward and deal with our issues even when we feel the Holy Spirit trying to work in us.

We miss out on so much power that way and by keeping those power blockers stuck in our blades. Those things grieve the Holy Spirit which we are told not to do in Ephesians 4:30.

We need to allow the breath of the Holy Spirit to go all the way through us so we can spin round and round doing the things Christ would have us to do.

*If we confess our sins, he is faithful and just to forgive us our sins, and to cleanse us from all unrighteousness. 1 John 1:9*

## So, how are you spinning?

# 17

# SUMMER KIND OF WONDERFUL

*Oh that men would praise the LORD for his
goodness, and for his wonderful works to the
children of men! Psalms 107:8*

**I** was glancing through one of my decorating
magazines and saw the title, *"Summer Kind of
Wonderful"* for one of the articles. I kept thinking
about that Bible verse that talks about God's
"wonderful works", so I looked it up and realized it
was in Psalm 107:8.

I then realized that the exact verse was repeated
four times in that Psalm. (107:8, 15, 21, 31)

*Oh that men would praise the LORD for his
goodness, and for his wonderful works to
the children of men!*

I do enjoy summer and began thinking of all the
*Summer Kind of Wonderful* things that the Lord

gives us. Let's take a look at some of them and see what we can learn.

## The Sun

Of course the first thing I think about in summer is the sun. I really missed the sunshine this winter. It was colder than usual here and I wanted so much for the sun to shine. I think the sun is such a fascinating thing. Only God could have made it.

The sun lights up the whole world and heats up the earth. It helps the crops grow. We can even use it as a power source.

The sun warms us up and does such good for our bodies. Overexposure to the sun can cause some health risks, but there are benefits from getting enough sunshine too. It is a source to help us produce Vitamin D for our bodies which we need. Sunshine sure helps our mood too and has such healing benefits.

I'm not going to look up all the facts of the sun for you but I'm sure you remember learning in school how phenomenally hot it is and how it's made up of different gases.

I think that the sun is such a wonderful and fascinating thing that God created.

> *The day is thine, the night also is thine: thou hast prepared the light and the sun. Psalm 74:16*

> *He appointed the moon for seasons: the sun knoweth his going down. Psalm 104:19*

## The Fruits and Vegetables

Summer to me means lots of fresh fruits and vegetables. Watermelon is my favorite summertime fruit. We haven't had one yet this year but I'm looking forward to biting into that first delicious cold slice of it for the summer.

I love getting fresh vegetables. We have corn on the cob throughout the year but I don't know why it tastes so much better in the summertime.

All those summer fruits and vegetables have so many things in them that benefit our health. They each have different vitamins that God made specifically for us for our nutrition.

*And God said, Behold, I have given you every*
*herb bearing seed, which is upon the face of all*
*the earth, and every tree, in the which is the fruit*
*of a tree yielding seed; to you it shall be*
*for meat.  Genesis 1:29*

## The Trees and Flowers

Another thing about summer is that everything is in full bloom.  The trees are full and green.  The flowers are in full bloom.  Summer is just a beautiful time of year.

We just got back from vacation and we travel partly through some hills that have trees scattered down the sides and it's just so beautiful.

There is one part we travel through with tall trees close to the road with branches hanging down that my kids starting calling the "Terabithia" part of the trip, which is a made up place from the *"Bridge to Terabithia"* movie.

I'm always struck with awe at God's creation as I look at the mountains in the distance and the trees when we travel that route every year.

*And God said, Let the earth bring forth grass, the herb yielding seed, and the fruit tree yielding fruit after his kind, whose seed is in itself, upon the earth: and it was so. And the earth brought forth grass, and herb yielding seed after his kind, and the tree yielding fruit, whose seed was in itself, after his kind: and God saw that it was good. Genesis 1:11, 12*

## The Ocean (ponds, rivers, and seas)

We usually spend a little time on vacation letting the kids run through the waves on the beach every year. As the water goes out, they scramble to find the sea shells that the waves brought up before the next wave comes in.

This year we skipped our beach time but I still enjoyed watching those waves roll in and out from a distance. You can't help but think of God and creation when you look at that water and remember all those creatures that you know it contains.

*And God said, Let the waters under the heaven be gathered together unto one place, and let the dry land appear: and it was so. And God called the dry land Earth; and the*

*gathering together of the waters called the Seas:*
*and God saw that it was good. Genesis 1: 9-10*

## The Bugs, Bees, and Insects

I'm not a big fan of all those bugs, bees and creepy insects, but God made each of them so wonderful and magnificent and I know I should appreciate how each one works its part. Each insect is full of intricacies and wonders that God built into them.

A few weeks ago there were so many bees around the front of our house. We had to be careful each time we opened and closed the front door. A few times I got stuck in my car until I was sure they were all gone from in front of the door and I'd make a mad dash into the house. I guess I can appreciate those things but I sure don't want them on me!

Recently my son was watching one of those bug shows on television and I caught myself just watching with interest their study of a praying mantis and I was thinking then just how fascinating it is how God made all those details to that little thing. I don't want one of those creatures on me either, but I know God has a purpose for its existence.

*And God said, Let the earth bring forth the living creature after his kind, cattle, and creeping thing, and beast of the earth after his kind: and it was so. And God made the beast of the earth after his kind, and cattle after their kind, and every thing that creepeth upon the earth after his kind: and God saw that it was good. Genesis 1:24-25*

## **Final Thoughts**

I always enjoy the start of a new season. It's fresh and new and it's amazing how we can see God's hand in it all around, but it's so easy to go about our day and not think about all those beautiful things the Lord has for us. I know I could appreciate all those "wonderful works" more.

Those verses in Psalm 107 say we should be praising God for His works and there are so many of them out there for us to enjoy.

God does so many more works than those in just creation but I think it's good to focus on those things once in a while, especially at the change of seasons.

*Many, O LORD my God, are thy wonderful works which thou hast done... Psalm 40:5*

*Thou hast set all the borders of the earth: thou hast made summer and winter. Psalm 74:17*

**So, will you be praising God for all of His wonderful works this summer?**

# 18

# DIAMONDS ARE
# A GIRL'S BEST FRIEND

*For ye were sometimes darkness, but now are ye light in*
*the Lord: walk as children of light. Ephesians 5:8*

Diamonds are wonderful things. As women, we like them. Of course we do! They sparkle. They shine. They are valuable. No wonder they are called our *best friend.*

I lost a lot of weight this past year and for several years before that I couldn't wear my wedding ring. It wouldn't fit because I had gained so much weight in my fingers. Only in the last several months since I lost weight have I been wearing my diamond.

I told my husband that it's just like I got it all over again and I really notice when it sparkles like I did when I first got married or something. I guess I'm just like a kid and enjoy that sparkle and the way the light hits it.

Diamonds are beautiful and when we are acting

like the Christian women God intended us to be, we can be beautiful too. We can sparkle and we can shine.

Diamonds don't start out beautiful. They come from deep in the earth. It's just like when we come to Christ for Salvation. We come from deep within the miry clay of sin.

One of the characteristics of a diamond is its clarity. That involves whether there is the presence of any impurities or inclusions in the diamond. Depending on its visibility, the grade of a diamond will go up or down.

As a Christian, any impurities in us will bring us down in grade as a Christian too. Others may not even see our impurities or our sins because it may not be visible with the naked eye, but remember that Christ can see our hearts. He knows what the scale of our *clarity* is.

Diamonds don't automatically shine and sparkle. Diamonds that are uncut are rough and aren't like the diamonds we wear in our jewelry. Only the cut diamonds sparkle.

A diamond has to be cut by someone who is skilled in diamond cutting for it to sparkle and reflect light. Only the cut Christian woman can sparkle too.

We as Christians have to be cut by our Master Designer in order to sparkle and reflect the light of Christ in the way that we should. An idea *cut* for a diamond causes all the light to be reflected back through the top of the diamond so that it reflects the maximum brilliance that it can.

When we allow Christ to mold us and to work in our lives and to *cut* the lines in us in the way that He as our Maker wants, then we reflect His light to the maximum in our lives.

If we are living that way and allowing Christ to mold us, there are some things that we will do if we are going to reflect Him in our lives.

## D - Delight in the Lord

*Delight thyself also in the LORD; and he shall give thee the desires of thine heart. Psalm 37:4*

# I - Increase in love.

*And the Lord make you to increase and abound in love one toward another, and toward all men, even as we do toward you. 1 Thessalonians 3:12*

# A - Abide in Christ.

*I am the vine, ye are the branches: He that abideth in me, and I in him, the same bringeth forth much fruit: for without me ye can do nothing. John 15:5*

# M - Minister to others.

*Distributing to the necessity of saints; given to hospitality. Romans 12:13*

# O - Obey God's Word.

*And hereby we do know that we know him, if we keep his commandments. 1 John 2:3*

# N - Never give up.

*Wherefore seeing we also are compassed about with so great a cloud of witnesses, let us lay aside every weight, and the sin which doth so easily beset us,*

*and let us run with patience the race that is set before us,*
*Looking unto Jesus the author and finisher of our faith;*
*who for the joy that was set before him endured the*
*cross, despising the shame, and is set down at the right*
*hand of the throne of God. Hebrews 12:1-2*

## D - Die to self.

*I am crucified with Christ: nevertheless I live; yet not*
*I, but Christ liveth in me: and the life which I now live*
*in the flesh I live by the faith of the Son of God, who*
*loved me, and gave himself for me. Galatians 2:20*

## <u>Final Thoughts</u>

Those diamonds sparkle and intrigue us and are something that we really admire as women, but just think about the light of Christ. How spectacular that is!

## So, how well do your sparkle?

# 19

# BEAT THE HEAT

*...the LORD is thy shade upon thy right hand. Psalm 121:5*

Here in California we are doing pretty good so far with the heat for the beginning of summer. It's only been in the low or mid 90's lately but pretty soon I know the summer heat will be unbearable. There are always things we can do though to cool off from the heat.

The heat of the world can beat down on us too. We've got to protect ourselves from it. Here are a few ways to beat the heat!

**Spend time in the shade.**

One of the first things we can do if we are outside and it is hot is to just get into the shade. As Christians, the best place to spend time in the shade is to spend time with the Lord in prayer and praise. We need to just sit at His feet and talk to Him. When we are there up close to the Lord it cools us down. The Lord protects us.

> The LORD is thy keeper: the LORD is thy shade upon thy right hand. The sun shall not smite thee by day, nor the moon by night. Psalm 121:5-6

## Hydrate yourself.

The next thing to do to cool off is to stay hydrated. We need to drink in lots of water. Here we are with all that heat of the world beating down on us and it takes so much out of us. It dries us out.

What better way to quench our thirst than by reading and studying the Word of God? We need to memorize it and really reflect on it for a while.

> As the hart panteth after the water brooks, so panteth my soul after thee, O God. My soul thirsteth for God, for the living God: when shall I come and appear before God? Psalm 42:1-2

> O God, thou art my God; early will I seek thee: my soul thirsteth for thee, my flesh longeth for thee in a dry and thirsty land, where no water is; Psalm 63:1

## Slow down.

When we are out in that heat just slowing down a little can help keep the sun from draining us. As Christians, we have to take the time to slow down and think before we get into trouble with our tongue and our actions. We don't want to become hot-headed.

*Wherefore, my beloved brethren, let every man be swift to hear, slow to speak, slow to wrath. James 1:19*

## Fan yourself.

We fan ourselves when it is hot to stir up the air. We feel cooler with a breeze hitting our faces. Just that little bit of air can revive you when it is hot.

Allowing the Holy Spirit to work in us can revive us too. When we allow the Holy Spirit to guide us it will strengthen us and give us that boost we need. It is then that we begin to feel the breeze.

*That he would grant you, according to the riches of his glory, to be strengthened with might by his Spirit in the inner man. Ephesians 3:16*

## Avoid strenuous activity.

When it is three digit temperatures out there it is not the best time to go doing all of the heavy labor things out of doors. We have to avoid that type of activity on days of extreme high heat. Those kind of conditions dehydrate us, strain our body, and make us weak.

What kind of things dehydrate us as Christians? What keeps us from reaching our full potential when it comes to serving Christ? There seems to be so many things that come blowing down on us with high heat that melts our spirits and makes us weary as Christians.

We especially have to avoid that extreme heat that we will experience when we get near sin. Sin will burn you.

*There hath no temptation taken you but such*
*as is common to man: but God is faithful, who*
*will not suffer you to be tempted above that ye are*
*able; but will with the temptation also make a*
*way to escape, that ye may be able to bear it.*
*1 Corinthians 10:13*

## **<u>Final Thoughts</u>**

We have all seen on the news what can happen when careless people leave their pets or even their children in extreme heat in a car. We cringe and wonder how anyone in their right mind could do that, but how careless are we with our lives? Do we expose ourselves to the extreme heat of sin?

I know I need to get in and cool out in the shade. I need to stay close to the Lord more; be refreshed with His word and allow the Lord to lead. I need that cooling off and lifting up that only Christ can give.

### **So, what are you doing to beat the heat?**

20

# IN LIKE A LION

*And they feared exceedingly, and said one to another,*
*What manner of man is this, that even the wind and*
*the sea obey him? Mark 4:41*

**I** am sure you've probably heard the saying, *in like a lion, out like a lamb* when referring to the month of March. In other words, if it starts out with cold weather, then by the end of the month, it starts warming up.

Of course we all know that doesn't always hold true but one of the reasons March comes in so fiercely cold is because of the wind. We normally think of March as the *windy month.*

Wind can be a lot of different things. It can be harsh, howling, cold or even gentle and calm. It all depends on how it is blowing at the moment. What I do know is that the Lord is in control of that wind.

*...What manner of man is this, that even*
*the wind and the sea obey him? Mark 4:41*

Let's look and see some ways that the Lord used the wind in the Bible.

### The Wind and the Rain (Genesis 8)

Noah and the Ark is a pretty well-known Bible story, so we'll start there. We know it rained for forty days and forty nights and we all know in the end that God stopped the rain, but have you ever noticed *how* He stopped the rain? He started with controlling the wind. Look at Genesis 8:1

*And God remembered Noah, and every living thing, and all the cattle that was with him in the ark: and God made a wind to pass over the earth, and the waters asswaged;*

I guess if I was Mrs. Noah I would be so thankful for that wind. I can't handle it when it rains for just a week, let alone forty days and forty nights.

### The Wind and the Chariots (Exodus 14)

In the story of Moses leading the Israelites from Egypt, God caused the water to be held back for the Israelites to pass through the Red Sea.

How did God hold all that water back? His command over the wind.

> *And Moses stretched out his hand over the sea; and the LORD caused the sea to go back by a strong east wind all that night, and made the sea dry land, and the waters were divided. And the children of Israel went into the midst of the sea upon the dry ground: and the waters were a wall unto them on their right hand, and on their left. Exodus 14:21-22*

## The Wind and the Quails (Numbers 11)

I learn so much from those Israelites and their journey around that wilderness and there's no better chapter to learn from than Numbers chapter 11. When I hear myself complaining, I try to remember this chapter. In the first verses of the chapter, the Israelites complain and God just burnt some of them up. It actually says "consumed". The people cried to Moses. Moses cried to God, and God stopped the fire.

A few verses later, here they go again with the complaining. They are hungry, but not for what's on the table for supper. My kids do that sometimes. They want anything other than what I've prepared for them. That's how the Israelites were in this passage. They want some meat to eat but God had prepared manna for them.

On down through the chapter you can read the interaction of the people, God, and Moses. Finally God taps into the that wonderful resource of His, the wind.

> *And there went forth a wind from the LORD, and brought quails from the sea, and let them fall by the camp, as it were a day's journey on this side, and as it were a day's journey on the other side, round about the camp, and as it were two cubits high upon the face of the earth. Numbers 11:31*

God gives them what they want but He is not pleased and the next thing you know, those complainers are hit with a plague while those quails are "yet between their teeth" (Numbers 11:33).

In verse 34 of that chapter you can see that they named that place, "Kibrothhattaavah" because that is where they buried the people that lusted.

This is the second time in the chapter that they had to stop and bury the dead of those that complained and displeased the Lord. I think most of us categorize complaining as a little thing but this is such a reminder that it is not a *little thing* after all.

**The Wind and the Fish** (Jonah 1)

Jonah being swallowed by a big fish is another story from the Bible that most people are familiar with, even those who are not Christians.

Here is Jonah, a man running from God. Well, he was trying to run anyway. It was a lesson he had to learn the hard way. Jonah hopped aboard a ship and went in the opposite direction that God wanted him to go, so God had to show Jonah that He knew exactly where Jonah was.

Again, God uses the wind.

*But the LORD sent out a great wind into the sea,*
*and there was a mighty tempest in the sea, so that*
*the ship was like to be broken. Jonah 1:4*

The next thing we know, Jonah is swallowed up by that fish and he's down in its stomach.  On into the next chapter of Jonah (Jonah 2:5) we see where he ended up.  Jonah landed down in the fish in the dark with water all around him and weeds wrapped around his head.  Not a very fun place to be and it was all because of Jonah's disobedience.

**The Wind and the Ship**  (Mark 4:35-41)

In this passage the disciples and the Lord are out on a boat.  Actually it says there were other "little ships" as well.  They had just left the multitudes so I imagine they were all tired and were looking forward to maybe relaxing a little out there on the water.

The Lord is asleep in the back of the ship and I can just imagine all of the disciples were just taking this time to unwind.  Then all of a sudden, here comes the wind.

*And there arose a great storm of wind, and the waves beat into the ship, so that it was now full.  Mark 4:37*

Here Jesus is sleeping and the disciples wake Him up. They are scared. The wind is making the waves fill up the ship with water. I love how it doesn't just say Jesus is asleep, but "asleep on a pillow". I'm not sure if it is exactly what we'd think of as a pillow, but it does tell me that Jesus was probably getting comfortable.

Jesus rebukes the wind just by speaking to it. Three little words. "Peace, be still" after which He questions the disciples about their faith.

*And he arose, and rebuked the wind, and said unto the sea, Peace, be still. And the wind ceased, and there was a great calm. Mark 4:39*

## Final Thoughts

In all of these stories from the Bible, we see lessons to be learned just by thinking about how God controlled the wind.

We all have a little wind that comes into our lives. Things that blow in when we least expect them. Other times they are things we know are coming but still they have an impact on us.

Sometimes that wind is fierce and howling. It can come in like a lion and freeze us to the bone. Sometimes the wind can knock us over like it does lawn furniture or it may be a little gentler with the force of simply blowing leaves into the air.

Sometimes the wind comes in the form of a tornado and lifts us up out of our comfort zone and plants us somewhere else and we get a little disoriented. Sometimes it blows dirt and debris into our eyes and we can't see what is up ahead. Other times that wind just cools us off in the summer sun. Still other times it is just so calming and gentle as it caresses us as we relax on the porch.

I'm so glad I know the Master of the wind. I know the One who controls when and if the wind will hit, with what force, and what the wind will bring with it in its wake. I'm so thankful that the Lord will be with me when the wind may hit me with a hard force or when it may come softly to my door.

**So, do you know the Master of the wind?**

## 21

# LANDING ON LILY PADS

*Trust in the LORD with all thine heart; and lean
not unto thine own understanding.  Proverbs 3:5*


Acrostics are a favorite thing of mine and I have
noticed the F.R.O.G. one is used a lot among
Christians.

**F**ully

**R**ely

**O**n

**G**od


I've seen it everywhere such as on bumper stickers
and I'm sure you have too.  That F.R.O.G. is kind of
a cute way to remember a good principle and I'm all
for anything simple like that which can help us in
our Christian walk.

I just hope that when we see a cute F.R.O.G. that
we don't forget that it represents serious business
for us as a Christian.  To fully rely on God is a big

thing for us. It's not a lighthearted thing. It is how we are to live as a Christian.

When we accept Christ, we give our lives over to Him. He is in control and we need to learn to rely on God and to rely on Him fully.

The definition of fully:
To the greatest degree or extent; completely or entirely.

The definition of rely:
Depend on with full trust or confidence.

I know I'm far from relying on God "fully" as I should, but as I started thinking about this I started reflecting about God and Who He is and how that in itself makes me want to rely on Him more.

I think we just need to get to know God better. We have an amazing God with amazing qualities. He offers us so much as His children. There are several things about our amazing God that I think may help us in our journey to rely on Him more.

I hope you'll come along with me as we go with the frogs and jump lily pad to lily pad. We're going to rest on each lily pad a little while we think about some of the things that will help us build up a reliance on the Lord.

Okay, ready to start hopping? Leap!

## The Lily Pad of God's Strength

We're landing here first because God's strength is one of those things that I need the most and *have* to rely on the Lord for in my life. Our own strength doesn't get us very far but when we're relying on the Lord's strength, look at how far we can leap.

*I can do all things through Christ which*
*strengtheneth me. Philippians 4:13*

*Finally, my brethren, be strong in the Lord,*
*and in the power of his might. Ephesians 6:10*

*Behold, God is my salvation; I will trust, and not be*
*afraid: for the LORD JEHOVAH is my strength and*
*my song; he also is become my salvation. Isaiah 12:2*

Much is said about Samson's strength, but it wasn't Samson's own strength that took down those pillars in the book of Judges (16:28-30). It was the strength of God that Samson prayed for.

I think about how David refers a lot to God's strength and how much he needed it for his life.

*The LORD is my light and my salvation; whom shall I fear? the LORD is the strength of my life; of whom shall I be afraid? Psalm 27:1*

Look how God encouraged the nation of Israel with His strength.

*Fear thou not; for I am with thee: be not dismayed; for I am thy God: I will strengthen thee; yea, I will help thee; yea, I will uphold thee with the right hand of my righteousness. Isaiah 41:10*

That's a mighty kind of strength that we can tap into and that we can rely on as we move along to our next lily pad. Ready? Hop!

## The Lily Pad of God's Love

We're just going to sit here on this lily pad for a bit and soak up some of God's love. It sure has a way of warming us up. It's that love that brought us to Christ in the first place. The Lord draws us to Him with His love so it's only fitting that we stop here and rest in that wonderful love for a while. It is a true and faithful love. It is one that we can rely on. It is a love that lasts.

*But God commendeth his love toward us, in that, while we were yet sinners, Christ died for us. Romans 5:8*

*The LORD hath appeared of old unto me, saying, Yea, I have loved thee with an everlasting love: therefore with lovingkindness have I drawn thee. Jeremiah 31:3*

*Who shall separate us from the love of Christ?... Romans 8:35*

Read the entire passage in Romans 8:35-39 to really get a grasp the concept of God's love.

When we know someone loves us, it helps us trust and rely on them more. It is the same with the Lord. We start thinking about His love and how can we not trust Him? He is never going to stop loving us.

I know people who have went through terrible

divorces. They say they just "don't love each other anymore". It is so nice to know we never have to worry that God will stop loving us. It is great that nothing can separate us from God's love either, so let's take it with us as we move along. Let's leap!

## The Lily Pad of God's Word

What a great place to land! Don't you love it when you can trust someone's word? You don't even need a handshake, let alone a contract. You just know you can trust what they say.

That is how it is with God. We never have to worry about Him ever breaking His Word. We can trust in that.

*For ever, O LORD, thy word is settle*
*in heaven. Psalm 119:89*

*For the word of God is quick, and powerful, and*
*sharper than any twoedged sword, piercing even*
*to the dividing asunder of soul and spirit, and of the*
*joints and marrow, and is a discerner of the*
*thoughts and intents of the heart. Hebrews 4:12*

God's Word is so dependable. I'm glad I don't have to wonder whether it's true or whether it will change or whether He will break it. I can go on along without even worrying about it.

Ready for our next leap? Let's go!

## The Lily Pad of God's Faithfulness

We have landed here so we can sit on this lily pad and think about God's faithfulness. It is pretty easy to trust and rely on people that are faithful. When someone's faithful, they are true to you. They show up. They are there for you. They are consistent. God's faithfulness to us is so much more than that.

> *Thy faithfulness is unto all generations: thou hast established the earth, and it abideth. Psalm 119:90*

> *It is of the LORD'S mercies that we are not consumed, because his compassions fail not. They are new every morning: great is thy faithfulness. Lamentations 3:22-23*

I am so glad that I have a faithful God that I can rely on. Knowing He is always going to be faithful makes me want to trust Him more.  I love that old hymn, *Great is Thy Faithfulness.*

*Great is Thy faithfulness!*
*Great is Thy faithfulness!*
*Morning by morning new mercies I see.*
*All I have needed Thy hand hath provided;*
*Great is Thy faithfulness, Lord, unto me!*
(Thomas Chisholm)

Sing with me as we leap to our next lily pad.  Hop!

**The Lily Pad of God's Wisdom**

Did you have a safe landing?  Sometimes I need to land here more often and think about God's wisdom.  It's so important.  God knows what He is doing.

It's funny how we will fully trust a professional's wisdom.  Sometimes they are complete strangers to us, but we trust their knowledge and wisdom that they specialize in, such as doctors, pilots, and business professionals.

We will put our life in their hands because we trust their training and that they know what they are doing. We wouldn't want to do our own surgery. Surely we wouldn't want to fly our own plane unless we were a pilot and trained for it.

We fully rely on these mere humans to do for us what we can't. We can trust a surgeon to cut us open and work on the intricacies of our bodies, knocked out unconscious with anesthesia, but sometimes it's hard for us to rely on the true and living God when we are fully awake.

We want to do the surgery ourselves and fly our own planes so to speak. Some people even trust professional advisers with their finances and allow them to make decisions on their behalf for their financial affairs but be afraid to trust God with their money.

God is so wise and in control of everything and yet we sometimes have trouble trusting God's plan for our lives.

*Now unto the King eternal, immortal, invisible,*
*the only wise God... 1 Timothy 1:17*

Why can't we trust God's wisdom more? His specialty is being a great and mighty God. Why do we find it so hard to trust that He knows what He's doing?

## **Final Thoughts**

When we have faith in and rely on other people, it's usually because we get to know them and what they are capable of. In ministry over the years, there have been ladies who I knew I could trust when they were given a task or something to do when working on a project.

They were those go-to people for me. They were the kind of people that always showed up, always did what was required, always followed through. We learn to know who we can and cannot rely on when we start spending more time with those people and getting to know them more.

It is the same way with God. We have got to start spending more time with Him and getting to know Him more. When we do, we learn that we can rely on Him. We can rely fully.

God is always going to show up for us, always going to be on time, always going to get the job done, always going to have good judgment, and always going to be faithful. The Lord is not going to let us down. He is the great go-to.

When the Jim Jones tragedy happened, I was a senior in high school. For those who are unfamiliar with that, he was a cult leader who gave his followers a poison filled drink which they willingly drank. There were close to 900 people that died.

At the time I had to do a current events notebook for a requirement for history class and it had to include newspaper clippings of current things from the news. I can remember cutting out those news articles with photos of all those body bags from the Jonestown tragedy and gluing them into my notebook. I'd never seen such a display of death.

I think we as adults and our children get immune to tragedies like that nowadays with 24 hour news channels, internet access, and so many true life television forensic shows and fictional ones as well.

When the Jonestown tragedy happened though, I

was young, and I had never seen anything like that on the local news or in the newspaper. I just couldn't wrap my head around how in the world all of these people could just follow a man like that to their death.

Thinking of it now, it must have been because they fully relied on that man. They put their whole lives in his hands. Jim Jones was just a man, a false leader who deceived people, yet so many people put their trust in him. We on the other hand have the true and living God. Why is this F.R.O.G. thing so difficult for us?

We have an amazing God that we can trust. We can trust His strength, love, Word, faithfulness, wisdom, and so much more. These lily pads we have landed on just represent *some* of the things to know about God that can help us rely on Him more, but there is so much above this about our great God that's worth finding out. There is so much more worth getting to know Him more.

I think when we start knowing God more and we start relying on Him more, it's also then that we begin seeing those great leaps of faith in our lives. Look at those faith heroes in the 11th chapter of Hebrews. Look at what those mere humans accomplished because they had faith in God, relied on Him, and trusted in Him.

When we don't rely on God fully, we sometimes end up staying on the edge of the pond. We end up sitting on a log somewhere. We never get out there and truly live the Christian life to its full capacity. Our lives don't end up where they should. Those leaps of faith seem insurmountable to us because we are trusting in ourselves or just in things.

*Trust in the LORD with all thine heart; and lean not unto thine own understanding. In all thy ways acknowledge him, and he shall direct thy paths. Proverbs 3:5,6*

I've challenged myself to get to know God better so I can work on this F.R.O.G. thing. I hope you will too. I'd like to be able to learn to trust and rely on God more and perhaps have some more leaps of faith.

Is there such a thing as a Watt Frog? I need a bumper sticker that says,

W.A.T.T. F.R.O.G.

**W**orking

**A**t

**T**rying

**T**o

**F**ully

**R**ely

**O**n

**G**od

**So, are you fully relying on God?** (or trying to)

# ABOUT THE AUTHOR

Julia Bettencourt is the *lady* behind Creative Ladies Ministry, which she began as a website in 2001 to share ministry ideas for leaders involved in women's ministry in the local church. Her devotionals quickly became the number one reason that people visit her website. Julia loves sharing the little lessons that she's learned in everyday life through her writing.

You can find Julia through her website where she shares ideas for women's ministry and blogs about what is happening in her home life.

www.juliabettencourt.com

Pastor's wives and women's leaders are invited to join her *Creative Ladies Ministry Facebook* Group to garner encouragement and to brainstorm ideas for women's ministry.

https://www.facebook.com/groups/juliabettencourt/

Julia lives in California with her family. She and her husband have been married for almost 36 years. They have three children.

Made in the
USA
Monee, IL